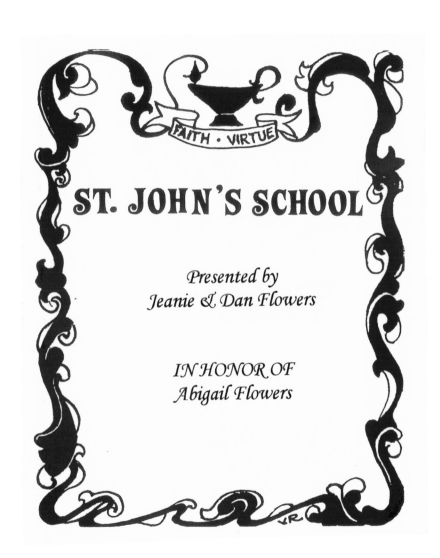

FAITH · VIRTUE

ST. JOHN'S SCHOOL

Presented by
Jeanie & Dan Flowers

IN HONOR OF
Abigail Flowers

Discovering
Cultures

Philippines

Sharon Gordon

BENCHMARK **B**OOKS

MARSHALL CAVENDISH
NEW YORK

With thanks to Stephen Graw, Development Sociologist, for the careful review of this manuscript.

Benchmark Books
Marshall Cavendish
99 White Plains Road
Tarrytown, New York 10591-9001
www.marshallcavendish.com

Library of Congress Cataloging-in-Publication Data

Gordon, Sharon.
Philippines / by Sharon Gordon.
p. cm. — (Discovering cultures)
Summary: Highlights the geography, people, food, schools, recreation, celebrations, and languages of the Philippines.
Includes bibliographical references and index.
ISBN 0-7614-1518-1
1. Philippines—Juvenile literature. [1. Philippines.] I. Title. II. Series.
DS655 .G66 2003
959.9—dc21   2002015304

Photo Research by Candlepants Incorporated

Cover Photo: Lucid Images/ Mark Downey

The photographs in this book are used by permission and through the courtesy of; *Lucid Images/Mark Downey*: 1, 4-5, 6, 8, 9, 10, 14, 15, 16, 17, 18, 20, 21, 23, 24, 27, 28 (both), 31, 33, 36, 37, 38, 39, 40, 41, back cover. *Corbis*: Paul A. Souders, 12, 19, 26, 30, 34; Abbie Enock:Travel Ink, 22; Dean Conger, 29; David Samuel Robbins, 32; Reuters NewMedia, 44 (right); Corbis, 44 (left). *Joan Marcus/Photofest*: 45.

Map and illustrations by Salvatore Murdocca
Book design by Virginia Pope

Cover: *Waterfall in the forest*; Title page: *A smiling young fisherman*

Printed in Hong Kong
1 3 5 6 4 2

Turn the Pages...

Mabuhay!

Mabuhay means "welcome" to a Filipino. So *mabuhay* to the beautiful islands of the Philippines!

Filipino friends with welcoming smiles

Where in the World Is the Philippines?

The Republic of the Philippines is an archipelago of islands in the southwest Pacific Ocean. It has been called the "Pearl of the Orient Sea" because on a map, the chain of islands looks like a beautiful necklace. The mountainous islands are part of Southeast Asia. They lie between the South China Sea on the west and the Pacific Ocean on the east. One of the deepest parts of the ocean is to the east of the Philippines. It is called the Philippine Trench. It is 6.2 miles (10 kilometers) to the bottom.

There are 7,107 islands in the Philippines, but people live on only about 1,000 of them. In fact, about 95 percent of the nation's population lives on eleven of

The island of Mindanao

6

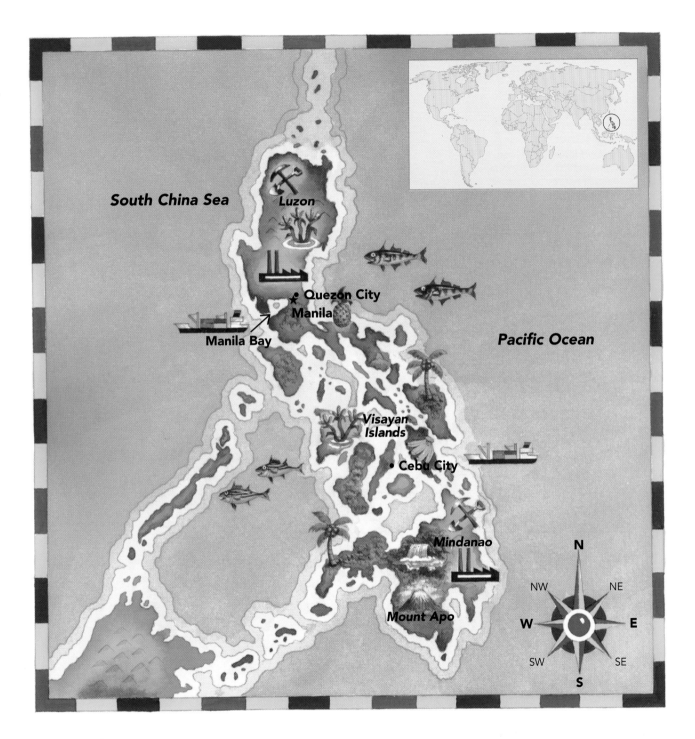

South China Sea

Luzon

Quezon City
★ Manila

Manila Bay

Pacific Ocean

Visayan
Islands

• Cebu City

Mindanao

Mount Apo

N
NW   NE
W   E
SW   SE
S

The capital city of Manila

the largest islands. Most of the islands are very small. Many have never been named. In total, the Philippines is about the size of the state of Arizona.

The islands of the Philippines can be divided into three general regions: Luzon, the Visayan Islands, and Mindanao. Luzon is the largest island at the northern end of the country. Two of the most important cities of the Philippines are located on Luzon: Manila, the capital, and nearby Quezon City. It is the center of Philippine government and business. Manila Bay is an important seaport.

The Visayan Islands are found in the center of the Philippines. Many crops such as rice, corn, sugarcane, sweet potatoes, coconuts, and small bananas are grown on these islands, providing food for the rest of the Philippines. Cebu City, on the island of Cebu, is a harbor and one of the Philippines' largest cities. It was a trading center as early as the sixteenth century. To this day, goods being shipped in and out of the central Philippines pass through Cebu City.

Mindanao is the second-largest island in the Philippines. Mount Apo, an active volcano and the highest mountain in the Philippines, is located on Mindanao. It

Cebu City's busy harbor

takes four or five days to climb to the top of Mount Apo. Besides high mountains, the island has green valleys, lush rain forests, and beautiful waterfalls. Farmers grow rice, sugarcane, pineapples, and coffee beans on Mindanao. Miners dig for nickel and iron.

The climate of the Philippines is warm and humid. The average temperature in the lowland areas is 80 degrees Fahrenheit (27 degrees Celsius), but it is cooler in the mountains. The weather changes with the direction of the monsoon winds. From November to May, the northeast monsoon brings warm, dry weather. But from June to October, the southwest monsoon brings a wet, rainy season. Each year during this time, the Philippine Islands are hit by five to twelve typhoons. These dangerous, slow-moving storms are known as hurricanes in the United States. They bring heavy

Rice paddies on a mountain

A smoking volcano on Luzon Island

rains, dangerous winds, and serious flooding. Some winds reach up to 150 miles (241 kilometers) per hour!

The Philippine Islands are within the Pacific Ring of Fire. This area has long been at high risk from volcanoes and earthquakes. Each year, the Philippines has many serious earthquakes. It also has several active volcanoes. Although volcanic eruptions can cause great damage, they help make rich soil for growing crops.

Mount Pinatubo

For 600 years, Mount Pinatubo sat quietly on the island of Luzon, with no volcanic activity. But then one hot day in June 1991, it erupted, spitting out fiery lava that spread over the land. It sent up ash and smoke 19 miles (30.5 kilometers) into the sky! Clouds of ash traveled as far as neighboring Indonesia and Singapore. Fine dust circled the whole world. The hot lava and flowing mud and rock destroyed villages and killed around 800 people. Thousands of others had to move away. Animals and crops were destroyed. Fortunately, scientists were able to predict the eruption and warn the people in the area to leave. They helped save at least 5,000 lives and millions of dollars in property.

What Makes the Philippines Filipino?

It is hard to describe a "typical" Filipino. The original islanders were mainly Malaysian and Indonesian. Then over the years, the Chinese, Japanese, Spanish, and Americans came to the islands. The Philippines became a meeting place of nations and cultures. As a result, there are about eighty ethnic groups having different languages and lifestyles and two major religions.

Despite their differences, Filipinos have many things in common. They are friendly. They are dedicated to their communities. They work very hard, but they also love to play. Filipinos have strong family ties. Many Filipinos live with grandparents,

People from many cultures live in the Philippines.

Parade marchers in traditional costumes

aunts, uncles, and cousins all in one house. If they do not live with their relatives, they visit each other often. Children are well loved and are taught to be respectful and obedient to their parents, relatives, godparents, neighbors, and friends. When Filipinos face a problem, they can turn to a network of relatives and close friends for help.

Children and teenagers in the Philippines dress very much like children everywhere. They might wear a T-shirt and jeans. On most days, a Filipino woman wears Western-style clothing. If there is an important party, she might put on more traditional Spanish-style clothes, like the Maria Clara, a long skirt and a soft blouse with a triangle scarf worn over the shoulders. Some women wear the ceremonial dress of their tribe. A Philippine man likes to dress casually. But to get dressed up, he might wear a Filipino shirt called Barong Tagalog. This dress shirt, made of pineapple or banana fibers, is not tucked in. It was first designed to help the ruling Spanish know who was a native and who was not.

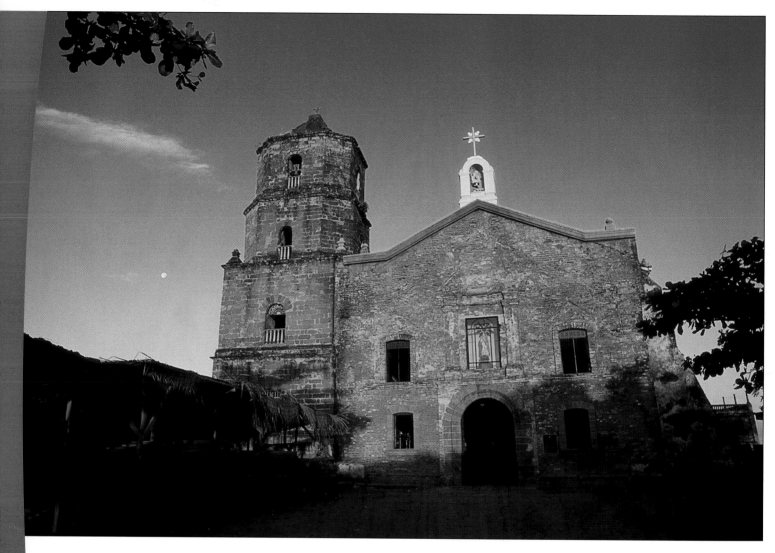

Many Filipinos attend a Catholic church.

The Philippines has two official languages: English and Pilipino, which was created in 1937 to unify the islands. It is based on the language of the Tagalog people who live on Luzon. English is spoken when conducting most business and government matters. The Philippines is the world's third-largest English-speaking nation. Still, most Filipinos continue to speak their local language.

Spain ruled the Philippines for about 300 years. The United States controlled the islands for about fifty years after the Filipinos drove out the Spanish. The Spanish had a great influence on the country. The islands were named after Spain's King Philip II. The Spanish brought their religion to the islands, and today, the Philippines is largely a Roman Catholic nation. Many Filipinos blend their native beliefs into their Catholic faith.

The Spanish were not able to conquer most native groups who lived in the mountains. Many of these people still live in isolation. Their clothing, music, language, and religion have not changed very much. Some pray to a rain god or an earth god. They might worship animals, trees, rocks, and *anitos* (ancestors).

Two hundred years before Europeans came to the Philippines, Muslim traders and missionaries arrived in the southern islands, especially Mindanao. The people on those islands still practice Islam today.

The music and art of the Philippines is diverse,

A member of a native tribe

Dancers wearing bright and colorful clothing

like its people. Filipinos enjoy ballet, musicals, and even rock music. The Cultural Center of the Philippines in Manila has three theaters for music, dance, and drama. Filipinos also enjoy the folk dances and music of their native tribes. Some weave colorful fabrics for their costumes. They might use native instruments such as the *kulintang*, a set of brass gongs from Mindanao. Through music, they pass on important traditions to their children.

The Coconut Palm

The coconut palm is one of the most important trees in the Philippines. Every part of the coconut palm is used for something. The leaves give shade from the sun. The nectar of its flowers can be made into a sweet drink. The coconuts themselves are eaten or used in cooking. Inside the coconut is a delicious juice. The dried shells are burned as fuel for cooking fires. Children love to climb up the coconut palm. And its sturdy trunk can be used for lumber, as well. No wonder the coconut palm is called the tree of life in the Philippines. It is an old custom for a family to plant a coconut palm as a symbol of new life whenever a child is born.

Living in the Philippines

Life in the Philippines can be very different, even within the same city. The capital, Manila, is as modern as any city in the United States. It has sprawling suburbs. It has tall skyscrapers. Many rich people live there in luxurious homes. But most sections of Manila are filled with poor people who cannot find work. They live in shacks. When bad weather comes, these people are at great risk of losing their homes and possessions. Rich or poor, city people have to deal with crowds, traffic jams, and pollution.

A crowded section of Manila

A village nipa *hut*

People living in hillside farming villages have simple homes. They live in one- or two-room *nipa* (thatched palm) huts, similar to those built hundreds of years ago. These houses are raised off the ground on stilts so that floodwaters cannot get inside. They are made of bamboo and wood. The roofs are made of a type of palm frond. Since there are no kitchens, meals are cooked and eaten outside— unless it rains!

Filipinos who live in cities might work for the government or in a factory making clothes. Some make computer parts or chemicals. Farmers live in the rural areas. They often grow rice, sugarcane, or coconuts. Fishing is another important industry. The ocean waters around the Philippines are rich in seafood. Fishermen live in the small villages along the coastline or next to lakes.

Big cities in the Philippines have large supermarkets, like in the United States. But many people still prefer to shop in open markets. They shop each day for fresh food. The people come in as early as 5:30 A.M. to buy their meat, vegetables, rice, and fruit.

Dinner is especially important to Filipinos. It is a time when family members can gather and share their experiences at the end of the day. If visitors arrive, they are invited to eat with the family. Rice is the most important Filipino food. Young

Fishermen set sail in their canoes.

Planting rice

children learn how to cook rice perfectly. It is eaten at every meal. And in some Filipino homes, it is not bad manners to eat with your fingers!

Filipino food is a mixture of cultures. Most dishes come from the Chinese and use soy sauce and noodles. From the Spanish come dishes with simmered meats and vegetables. Of course, for those who live in cities, fast-food restaurants are everywhere! Filipinos love pizza and burgers as much as Americans. The most successful fast-food chain in the Philippines serves burgers, hot dogs, and shakes but flavors them with local seasonings.

You know you are in the Philippines if you see a *jeepney*. It is a cross between a jeep and a bus. After World War II, American soldiers left behind hundreds of jeeps. The Filipinos turned these old jeeps into buses and used them for public transportation in the cities. The people loved them so much, they built bigger and better ones to replace them. They put in large benches for passengers. They painted and decorated them in bright colors. Today there are more than thirty thousand *jeepneys* in use throughout the islands.

Riding in a jeepney

24

Let's Eat!
Champorado

Champorado is a chocolate rice pudding. Ask an adult to help you prepare this popular Filipino breakfast.

Ingredients:

$1/2$ cup long-grain rice
(not instant or converted)

2 cups water

8 tablespoons cocoa or
unsweetened cocoa powder

4 teaspoons sugar

Milk or sweetened
condensed milk

Wash your hands. Rinse the rice. Put the rice and water in a covered pan and simmer over medium heat until the rice is soft. Remove from heat and add the cocoa and sugar. Mix well. Serve in a bowl with milk or sweetened condensed milk. Makes four servings.

School Days

Helping out on the farm

Education is very important to the people of the Philippines. Students who do well bring honor to their families and give their parents hope for the future. Filipino children can attend public school for ten years: six in elementary school and four in high school. They must go to school until they have completed the sixth grade. But more than half of Filipino children continue through high school. The parents of many poor children cannot afford to keep them in school. These children must go to work to help support their families. Some work in businesses or factories or at the market. Others work full-time on the family farm or help their parents with housework.

Students who attend private schools wear uniforms. Some public school students and their teachers

The beginning of a school day

wear uniforms, too. The school year goes from June to March, five days a week. It is too hot in April and May to study! The school day begins at 7:30 A.M. by raising the flag and singing the national anthem. Children study all morning, take an hour for lunch, and then go back to classes until mid-afternoon. It is a long day and the students study hard. The classrooms are large and airy. Usually there is an open space outside for children to play.

The Philippines has a high literacy rate, which means most of the people can read and write. In elementary school, students learn math, science, history, reading, and many of the same subjects that children study in the United States. In addition, they are taught about the different native cultures of the Philippines. They also learn practical skills, such as sewing and cooking. Classes are generally taught in English. Many students have homework. After school, students are also expected to help their families with chores around the house.

A student hard at work

Some Filipino students continue their education at a public or private college. Many attend the University of the Philippines in Quezon City. It is the country's largest public university. Others go to the 400-year-old University of Santo Tomas, a private Catholic college. It is the oldest university in Asia. It was founded in 1611. It is named after Saint Thomas Aquinas, the patron saint of Catholic schools. There are also many new, small private schools that offer classes in computer programming, automobile and airplane repair, and even cooking and baking.

Time to have fun with friends

Pedicabs

Children in villages might ride to school in a pedicab instead of a school bus. A pedicab is a bicycle or motorcycle with a wide, covered passenger seat attached to its side. A pedicab has three wheels, so Filipinos call these pedicabs tricycles. Seven or eight students sometimes squeeze into the tricycle. Some ride on the back bumper while they are driven over the rough country roads. Riding in a pedicab makes going to school quite an adventure!

Just for Fun

People who live in large Filipino cities relax in the same ways as people living in the United States. They go shopping in giant malls or go to flea markets to find bargains. They also go to movies, dance halls, or museums. They watch their favorite television shows and soap operas. They sit outside and visit with neighbors. Many families have computers and surf the Internet.

A teenager takes a break from rollerskating.

Weaving a basket

In rural areas, family activities depend on the weather. During the rainy season from June to October, people look for things to do inside, such as watching television, playing games, or making *buli* (wicker baskets). Many Filipinos are skilled at weaving beautiful baskets in all shapes and sizes. When the good weather comes, rural neighbors enjoy outdoor picnics and children play games in the street or on the basketball court. Families gather to share news or tell stories.

For vacation, city people head to islands that have beautiful beaches for sailing, swimming, or fishing. Others travel into the cool mountains to enjoy the fresh air and beautiful views. People who live in rural areas enjoy visiting the big cities during their vacation. They tour the museums in Manila and learn about their history. They enjoy shopping and visiting important Philippine landmarks, such as Rizal Park. This park is named after José Rizal, a famous Filipino hero. The park contains the Rizal Monument, the National Library, the Planetarium, and the Aquarium. It also has a playground and skating rink. Filipinos of all ages often travel to holy places to pray at the shrines of saints and miracle workers.

Americans brought the game of basketball to the Philippines. It has become Filipinos' favorite sport. Both children and adults love the game! Almost every town and village has a bas-

The Rizal Monument

ketball court. If not, children make their own hoops and tie them to poles or trees. Filipinos play basketball with great speed and timing. Their professional teams are well loved. They play throughout Asia. During a championship game, the whole nation seems to stop and watch.

Another favorite pastime of the Philippines is a sport called *sabong* (cockfighting). Filipinos have enjoyed *sabong* for hundreds of years. It is second in popularity to basketball, but it is a bloody sport. In *sabong*, trained roosters wearing small knives on their feet fight each other. The people in the audience cheer them on and bet

Shooting hoops

33

which bird will win the fight. The Catholic Church is opposed to *sabong*, but the Philippine government passed a law making these fights legal. While the adults watch the roosters fight, children have spider or beetle fights.

A prize rooster

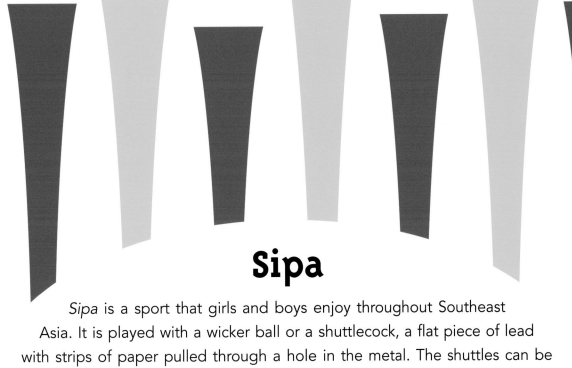

Sipa

Sipa is a sport that girls and boys enjoy throughout Southeast Asia. It is played with a wicker ball or a shuttlecock, a flat piece of lead with strips of paper pulled through a hole in the metal. The shuttles can be bought in a store or made at home. In the country, children make shuttles out of strips of palm leaves. The fluffier the ends, the better the shuttle will stay in the air. To play *sipa*, children kick the ball or shuttle with their feet, heels, or toes. They try to keep it up in the air without touching it with their hands. Each kick is worth one point. A good *sipa* player can score one hundred points or more. The game can be played alone or in teams.

Let's Celebrate!

Waving the flag at a parade

Filipinos love to celebrate. They gather with friends and family to enjoy good food and company during *fiestas* (festivals) and holidays. They hold parades and have fireworks. Some holidays are religious. Others remember important days in Philippine history, such as Independence Day on June 12. That marks the day in 1898 when General Emilio Aguinaldo, a Filipino revolutionary, declared the islands free from Spain.

Christmas is a long and happy Christian festival in the Philippines. Most Filipino families decorate the outsides of their homes instead of the insides. They hang beautifully decorated star-shaped lanterns, called *parols*, that light up the dark evenings. They put up flags and colorful flowers.

Christmas lights at night

The Filipino Christmas celebration starts at dawn on December 16, when the Christmas story is read at a special Catholic mass called the Misa de Gallo (Mass of the Rooster). On Christmas Eve, plays retell the story of the birth of Jesus. Most families attend special church services on Christmas Day.

A church decorated for the holidays

The festivities continue with the arrival of the New Year. Filipinos celebrate by making a lot of noise. They bang pots and pans, light firecrackers, and blow horns. The Christmas season ends on January 6 with the Feast of the Epiphany, also called the Feast of the Three Kings.

Holy Week is an important time for Filipino Christians. They remember the suffering and death of Jesus Christ. Holy Week begins with Palm Sunday. People wave palm branches, and hang them in their doors and windows. During Holy Week, Filipinos observe Good Friday. Sometimes they walk through the streets with wooden crosses on their shoulders. Holy Week ends with special religious services on Easter Sunday.

Other Philippine festivals honor patron saints, or protective spirits. Farmers honor their patron saint during the harvest season. They give thanks for their successful crops. Their celebration might include parades, marching bands, floats, singing and dancing, and always lots of good food! At many important festivals,

Observing Good Friday

Dressed for a harvest festival parade

lechon (roasted pig) is served. It is stuffed with spices and slowly roasted over coals. Then the cooked pig is displayed in the middle of the table. What a centerpiece!

Muslims living on the island of Mindanao celebrate a religious holiday called Ramadan. Ramadan is a twenty-nine-day-long fast during the ninth month of the Muslim calendar. During Ramadan, Muslims are not allowed to eat anything from sunrise to sunset. Even schoolchildren do not eat or drink during these hours.

Hari Raya Puasa is a great thanksgiving feast that marks the end of Ramadan. Young men go through the villages at dawn to beat drums, telling people that the fast is over and the festival has begun. Dancers and musicians fill the streets. Delicious food is served in Muslim homes and children receive gifts. Families relax and visit friends and relatives.

Parols

The *parol* is one of the greatest symbols of Christmas in the Philippines. These star-shaped lanterns decorate homes, restaurants, hotels, and stores throughout the islands. They light the dark nights in the streets of large cities and small villages. The *parol* represents the star that guided the Three Wise Men to the manger in Bethlehem where Jesus was born. The word *parol* is from the Spanish word meaning "lantern." It is believed that *parols* were first used to light the way to church for the Misa de Gallo service on December 16th. *Parols* have become a Filipino folk craft and even young children make simple ones from bamboo sticks, paper, glue, and candles. *Parols* are also sometimes made from local materials, such as coconuts or shells. Huge twenty-foot *parols* with flashing electric lights are paraded down the streets in the city of San Fernando on Luzon.

The national flag of the Philippines was adopted in 1898, when the Philippine Islands declared their independence from Spain. The red band stands for courage and the blue for noble values. During peacetime, the red band is on the bottom and the blue on the top. During war, the colors are reversed. The white triangle stands for the country's struggle for freedom from Spain. The yellow sun in the center of the triangle stands for liberty. The eight provinces that first fought for freedom are represented by the eight rays of the sun. In the corners of the triangle are three smaller stars, representing the three main regions of the Philippines.

The peso is the main currency of the Philippines. Pesos come in coins and banknotes, or paper money. The banknotes have pictures of Philippine leaders or important buildings. The exchange rate changes often, but in 2002 one U.S. dollar equaled approximately 53 pesos.

Count in Pilipino

English	Pilipino	Say it like this:
one	isa	EE-sah
two	dalawa	da-la-WA
three	tatlo	tot-LOW
four	apat	ah-POT
five	lima	lee-MA
six	anim	ah-NEEM
seven	pito	pee-TOW
eight	walo	wa-LOW
nine	siyam	SHAHM
ten	sampu	sahm-POO

Glossary

adobo (ah-DOH-boh)   Meat or fish marinated in vinegar, soy sauce, garlic, and spices.

anitos (ah-NEE-tohs)   Spirits of ancestors worshiped by early Filipinos.

archipelago   Group of islands in the sea.

Epiphany   Feast of the Three Kings; celebrated on January 6.

frond   Leaf from a palm tree.

lechon (LECH-tsone)   Roasted suckling pig.

mabuhay (ma-BOO-high)   "Welcome" in Pilipino.

monsoon   Strong seasonal wind from the ocean that brings heavy rains.

republic   Nation where citizens vote for their government representatives.

sabong (SAH-bong)   Cockfighting.

Proud to Be Filipino

Maria Corazon Aquino (1933–   )

Corazon Aquino was the wife of Filipino politician Benigno Aquino. Together they had five children. Benigno Aquino did not agree with the policies of former Philippine president Ferdinand Marcos. In 1980, President Marcos exiled Benigno to the United States. When Benigno returned to Manila in 1983, he was killed. In 1985, Corazon decided to continue her husband's work to restore democracy to the Philippines. Even though she had no political experience, Corazon ran for president. She had the strong support of the people. In 1986, Corazon Aquino became the first woman president of the Republic of the Philippines. She made many social and economic reforms. Corazon is often used as an example of what women can do in Philippine society. *Time* magazine named her their Woman of the Year in 1987.

José Rizal (1861–1896)

Dr. José Rizal was an author, poet, and Philippine hero. He wrote two great novels about the cruelty of Spanish rule and the noble character of his countrymen.

As a young man, he studied to become a doctor at Philippine and European universities. In 1886, Rizal wrote a book about Spain's harsh treatment of the Filipinos. He returned to Manila and started the Filipino League in 1892 to help stop these abuses. Rizal gave the people hope that they would one day be free. He became a leader in the fight for independence from Spain. Because of this, he was forced to leave Manila and was ordered to live in Mindanao. In 1896, he was arrested and put to death for his revolutionary ideas. However, instead of stopping the independence movement, his death made it grow stronger.

Lea Salonga (1971–)

Lea Salonga is one of the Philippines best-known singers and entertainers. She was born and educated in Manila. Salonga began her career at the age of seven in the Repertory Philippines' production of *The King and I*. She starred in the musical *Miss Saigon* from 1989 to 1992, for which she won an Olivier Award and a Tony Award. Salonga is the voice of Jasmine in the Disney movie *Aladdin* and the lead singing voice in *Mulan*, another Disney movie. She has recorded many popular albums and performed both in the United States and the Philippines. In addition to her work as an actress and performer, Lea Salonga studied at Fordham University in New York City.

Find Out More

Books

Children of the Philippines by Sheila Kinkade. Carolrhoda Books, Minnesota, 1996.

Countries of the World: The Philippines by Joaquin L. Gonzalez III. Gareth Stevens Publishing, Wisconsin, 2001.

Enchantment of the World: The Philippines by Walter G. Olesky. Children's Press, New York, 2000.

The Philippines, Pacific Crossroads by Margaret Sullivan. Dillon Press, New York, 1993.

Web sites

http://www.yahooligans.com/around_the_world/countries/philippines/
Links to photographs and maps of the Philippines, plus numerous sites on the country's culture and history.

http://sunsite.berkeley.edu/KidsClick!
Type in *Philippines* and search the Web.

Videos

The Philippines: Pearls of the Pacific. International Video Network Entertainment, 1996. 57 min.

Index

Page numbers for illustrations are in **boldface.**

About the Author

Sharon Gordon has written many nature and science books for young children. Previously she worked as an advertising copywriter and a book club editor. She is writing other books for the Discovering Cultures series. Sharon and her husband Bruce have three teenage children, Douglas, Katie, and Laura, and one spoiled pooch, Samantha. They live in Midland Park, New Jersey. The family especially enjoys traveling to the Outer Banks of North Carolina. After she puts her three children through college, Sharon hopes to visit the many exciting places she has come to love through her writing and research.